IN LIVING MEMORIES

Poems by Anupam Banerjee

COMPOSITIONS

"It was at that age, that poetry came in search of me." – Pablo Neruda

Joshimath

A hill station in Uttarakhand which hosts glacial air enthused with the medicinal oils from alpine forests and the sweet texture of honey from wild bees nesting on Rhododendron flowers.

The clear blue sky provides the perfect backdrop for the Himalayas wide open in front of you to ski, climb or be enamored with just watching the beautiful landscape.

This is the story of Bholu, a Himalayan Mastiff Dog. He was a gift from the Head Man of Mana, the last village of India. In his short life of adventures and fun, he left behind a precious story.

Bholu

It was a rainy day when they brought you in,

My eyes lit up as I saw your fluffy face.

You circled our house sniffing and digging,

To determine your spot and favorite place.

I always wondered if you smiled through your eyes,

In all your mischief, every day you gave us a surprise.

Your excitement when I threw the Frisbee far ahead,

You ran as fast as you could on the green grass spread.

IN LIVING MEMORIES

I remember watching those sunsets behind the pine trees,
While you searched for chestnuts, cones, and berries.
It became so integral to have you in every trip we made,
The long walks in the forest and every new path we laid.
You walked ahead of us sniffing for any bygone trails,
Showing us forest mushrooms, wild langurs and snails.

On wintry nights when our fireplace had chestnuts baking,
You sat in for our sessions of laughing and storytelling.
Then one day we woke up and saw that you were in pain,
Three months young, you whined as I caressed your mane.
Upon examination, the doctor confirmed you contracted Polio,
But he gave you a pat, a biscuit and said you are a real Hero.
So, every morning we travelled those pathways downhill,
The doctor always treated you with tender love and goodwill.
He always told you are brave and you will be healthy soon,
A cake was a reward for sitting quiet, sometimes till noon.

In a few months we received good news on a sunny day,
You were healthy now and the medications went away.
We were delighted after knowing this so we celebrated,
Music, cake, balloons, and your room were decorated.

In a year you grew to be big like a bear,
Black and tanned with thick long hair.
A serious face and a fearsome bark shaking the surrounding,
You chased and pounced on rats but they always escaped your huge paws dancing.
Because they understood that you were their enemy but a friend,
Someone who meant no harm and they can easily comprehend.
One of your friends was 'Bunty,' a small Pariah from the streets,
You loved carrying croissants for him and give him little treats.
You felt compassion for your friend not living the life you do,

On our car rides, if you saw him, you pushed us to take him too.

He would jump in joy whenever he saw you,

With expectant and happy eyes, he waited for you.

Then a day arrived that our transfer from Joshimath was announced,

The grief was inexplicable and the feeling of farewell was pronounced.

Seeing us all in a pensive state you were curious but did not know why,

You still played with Bunty without foreseeing the upcoming goodbye.

We were transferred to another town and we had to leave soon,

In 'doggy' words and gestures we explained you this one afternoon.

You tried to understand us with your head bobbing side to side,

Your ears in full attention and your eyes open wide.

We felt you understood something through our tone,

The sadness and our journey towards the unknown.

Those days you rested most of the time as if thinking,

We brought your favorite munchies, but you were sinking.

Then one morning we just realized what we were to do,

We set out in our car around the hills to look through.

Back by the evening eagerly wanting to surprise you,

We heard you howling as we saw you in rear view.

There was not one but two dogs howling,

It was something which got you sparkling.

From the back of our jeep, Bunty jumped out,

He leaped towards you with a huge shout.

We still have this moment captured of you feeling surprised,

Your happiness knew no bounds as your friend arrived.

We let you be with him as you would not leave him,

Running around the garden and enjoying a puddle swim.

The day arrived when we had to leave the next morning,

All our belongings packed; our house was in mourning.

Bunty could not understand what was happening,

But he gave you company and prevented you from grieving.

With final preparations done we all sat in the car,

You were in the middle seat and Bunty stood afar.

At that moment, we saw the way both of you gazed at each other,

It was a bond of great friendship which had prospered.

As we moved ahead, we heard Bunty howling and crying,

You were equally affected and you also started crying.

As the wheels of the car rolled ahead in motion,

Bunty chased behind us with frenzied emotion.

Something struck us deep inside at that moment,

We stopped the car as we all felt stuck and frozen.

It was as if no discussions were needed to decide what to do,

We instinctively knew what we needed to do for both of you.

So, I got out, picked Bunty, and brought him inside to you,

He leaped to hug you to express how much he loves you.

Bunty was coming with us to wherever we were going,

He had a new home, a new family, and a new beginning.

10 years later

Here I am today lying in my bed flipping the photo album,

All your moods, expressions, and eyes full of enthusiasm.

You still live with us in our memories, and we often remember you,

Bunty still waits for you at Lunch and sometimes he does not eat too.

We accepted your departure as one of nature's laws,

But we miss playing with your whiskers and huge paws.

Your secret games of stealing croissants for Bunty every day,

Spending hours in the mud and endless tricks you played.

As time went by Bunty became a constant reminder of you,

You were fortunate to have a loyal friend who still thinks of you.

One some evenings I still throw the frisbee far ahead in the blue skies,

Hoping that one day you will catch it and bring me a surprise.

IN LIVING MEMORIES

Your place in the bed is still vacant as Bunty preserves it for you,

At night before sleeping, he licks the pillow which had you.

We keep seeing your photographs but cannot speak much as words do not allow us to,

A deep spot in our heart just feels good that you received as much love as you deserved to.

You still live on with us in our heart and this is an ode written for you,

Our heart resounds with special songs whenever we remember our dear 'Bholu'.

Its Five pm and a cone from the pine tree rolls towards me on this dangerous slant of the mountain. Far down below in the meadow, children wearing blue school sweaters are playing football. This football is from the Army barracks, carrying no air but a hope that if the boys kick hard it will reach towards the goal post and so they chase the slow rolling ball. Their innocent faces without comparisons to others are pure and free.

Happiness

Amongst the pine trees travels a breeze,

Vagrant in nature, it settles on my knees.

Lying down watching far into the sky,

The sun shines on and the birds fly.

I have been feeling these feelings,

Of nothingness in my head.

Where there are no plans,

Just watching the sunrise and sunset.

My friend, Vinod, has a smile on his sculpted face,

His goats wear tinkle bells and walk in a slow pace.

He owns a small restaurant in the town,

And lives in a cottage with flowers all around.

I remember the days in our high school,
Days spent studying atoms and molecules.
It is a different world outside they say,
We do not care; we will be ready one day.
Sometimes the pine cones beckon us to tread,
And we discover a rainbow lit valley ahead.
The same questions arise in our mind,
How nature is so planned and refined.
How the mountain road cuts inward;
And how the grasslands expand unhindered;
These small houses built on mountain slopes;
The bridge on the gushing river made with planks and ropes.

I hear a jeep and look behind me,
The driver says he has space and invites me.
We get inside the car and join the passengers,
They watch ahead fixedly carrying canisters.
Shopping for vegetables done and they are thinking about the night,

They will sit around the wood fired Chulha and prepare Saag tonight.

Fresh vegetables, Roti, and chutney from the garden,

They will chat about the world and their day's bargain.

Early morning the rooster will wake them up at five,

Trusting that, they will pray and feel thankful to be alive.

***

The classrooms of my school were army bunkers, converted to a school. Amongst snowfall and rain, the classes took place every day. Our class had 15 students. Some of them travelled one hour on foot to reach the school and go back as their village had no cars.

One of the stories is of my friend, Kamal.

Those days in the mountains

In your eyes are stories embedded so deep,

Of life spent walking up the hills so steep.

The fresh morning stack of wood to be used in the evening,

A charcoal flavored food with medicinal herbs as seasoning.

While fanning the flame and putting diligent effort,

A simmering sound and crackle are all that is heard.

Pahadi Rajma, Bichhu Buti Saag and Tamatar chutney,

A smoke-filled earthen kitchen which has no chimney.

The dusk has set in, there are sounds of footsteps from the forest,

Guests are expected tonight and you set up warm beds for their rest.

After dinner, everyone gets ready to play cards sipping tea,

Prepared on wood fire, the tea has ginger and honey.

Next morning, before dawn you had to attend to your hens,

Their trusting faces certain you are protecting their pens.

With a simple breakfast of Roti and Dal we set out again,

Seeming to know the destination but to get lost again.

I remember our hike up in the mountains,

The sunlit snow peaks and ice fountains.

Your dog 'Sheru' accompanied us on the way,

Three of us walking on this snow-clad day.

I was thinking about the conversations we had last night,

Listening to the sound of the rain was a great delight.

Fifteen years later

It's been fifteen years since and I have travelled all the way to meet you,

Walking up the pathways, passing waterfalls and the Himalayan view.

I waited for you to come back as they told me you had gone somewhere,

The house still looked the same perhaps needing a paint job and repair.

Just then I saw you waving towards me from a distance and laughing,

You still looked the same, a bit older, but very much obliging.

A tough mountain life and the weight of logs on your shoulders,

Your kids helped you with the load and set aside the boulders.

Life did not change you as I saw the same smile on your face,

You asked me if I was comfortable as you took me to the fireplace.

Then we sat talking about all that happened in these past years,

You brushed away topics saying everything is fine and you have no fears.

You are a mountain farmer now selling Ginger, Oranges and Prunes,

You listened keenly about my idea to also grow mountain Mushrooms.

I tried giving some money to fix the roof of your house which you did not accept.

It was a mud floor where you and your family of five slept.

I wondered what arrangements you did for the rain if it seeps through the roof,

But it is the mountain life of many and you must have made your house rain-proof.

You loaded me with fruits and vegetables as gifts to take back home,

A family so generous with such a big heart they own.

As I walked up the hill thinking of your life that I could see,

Flashes of memory and melancholy started enveloping me.

The pathways and the mountains reminded me of our time,

The frozen streams and snow, an experience of a lifetime.

Sensing that your family had a few things but were content,

Short summers or extended winters, both had your consent.

Your family offered happiness to everyone around you,

Even the birds and animals shared a safe shelter with you.

The simplicity of your life is what made it hard to understand,

Without so many needs and desires and a life unplanned.

These are contrasts which I can see in our lives,

As for some, there is never enough in our lives;

And for some there is enough for all our lives.

Would you believe if I tell you?

I would pay anything to live in these mountains today.

Nothing in my city compares to this;

There is nowhere that I find such places to stay.

I realized that the secret is to be simply content where you are,

There is enough for your need and happiness is not afar.

***

Mussoorie

The name itself strikes a happy chord in our mind. Some remember it as a destination they visited during summers and for some, its home to one of the best writers that the world has produced.

For me, Mussoorie is also a land that remains undiscovered. There were not many people visiting Char Dukan and Sister bazaar when I started visiting. Now there are Cafes in that remote place where once there were just a few houses and the mountains ahead.

A great congregation of culture, beauty, and stories – Mussoorie.

A Sunday morning. The tick tock of the horses down in the Camel back road, the distant horn of a car and a day that does not have a plan.

Raju was a house help and a friend.

Morning Reflections

I opened my eyes and looked at everything around me,

Warm rays from the Sun touching and surrounding me.

It was one hour past since the alarm last rang at seven.

I snoozed the alarm and an extra hour felt like heaven.

In my partial sleep I heard Raju calling me several times,

No name for my non-response, I call these 'lazy times.'

He understood that I woke up as he came in with our tea,

He reminded me that it was I who asked him to awake me.

Last night we discussed the habit of waking up early,

And that we wanted to be Wise, Wealthy and Healthy.

These mornings are special as the tea and sunshine seem a treasure.

A mild stretch of the arms and fingers, sipping tea in measure.

Then from a distance arrived a beautiful little bird singing at my window,

A sunny morning in Mussoorie and the squirrels peeping out from their burrow.

The backdrop of the mountains from my window beckoned me,

To come and look far across the sunlit valley feeling free.

I have been enamored with the history of this beautiful hill station,

Colonial buildings stand as glorious heritage for this generation.

How long have these rocks been silently around in this small town,

How many people like me have thought the same looking around?

In the past ten years houses have grown in numbers covering the hills,

The mountains make space for the houses and people with special skills.

The trees are always generous providing shelter and peace to everyone,

Birds and animals rest in their shade and travelers find relief from the Sun.

Where have the quiet roads of the past disappeared as every turning has a car?

Is there any place left where it feels as serene as Char dukan and Sister Bazaar?

Landour has become a busy tourist spot where everyone wants to be treading,

Reading books about Mussoorie and matching their description in the spreading.

IN LIVING MEMORIES

The other day I was at the book stall in Mall Road
watching people walk by,

It was different years back when there was quietness in
the month of July.

The benches were always inviting us to keep sitting and
watching the landscape,

With tea in our hands, talking about the afternoon rains
and places to escape.

We are lucky that we saw the difference between then
and now,

We old timers know our hideouts well and protect them
with a vow.

There are secret places around this small town that no one
knows,

An old colonial bungalow with a fireplace, perfect for
when it snows.

Let us get back to our morning duties and wait for the
evening walk,

Its Autumn and today we will walk far south to hear a
special talk.

We will be going to a village and having our dinner at Mahesh's home,

On the way we will see pine trees, mulberries and pick a conifer cone.

There is still some snow spread around the village from the bygone winter,

We will listen to age old stories and set up their fire place with splinter.

***

What are the words you can think of when you see a beautiful bird sitting at your window and looking at you?

For me it is 'Serenity.'

Describing this bird, I saw closely

A flap of feathers was heard at my window,

My eyes touched a glimpse of the far meadow.

You flew in panting with your beak open,

One glance at me, was your gratitude token.

As I marveled at your beauty and simplicity,

I stepped ahead to be closer to your white positivity.

You flew away into a circle in the backdrop of the blue sky,

Twisting and turning in your happiness letting everything go by.

Then you flew back in and sat at my window again,

I offered you a few walnuts and some pieces of grain.

This became a regular phenomenon to see you every day,

Laying food at my window and waiting the same way.

IN LIVING MEMORIES

You brought in a lot of joy through the splendor of your colors,

As I saw into your innocent eyes, your happiness did me wonders.

I brought out my canvas board one day to reflect you in paint,

The best of colors laid out and preparation to prevent from taint.

Finishing the painting, with the last few strokes I thought,

I am not satisfied with the range of colors I sought.

I tried to imagine ways of how I can get this picture right,

Why this painting does not resemble you in your exact white.

After some thinking a revelation deemed on me,

Nature cannot be replicated artificially by me.

It must be seen with my eyes and felt through my heart,

Nature itself paints the feelings which does not depart.

Even with closed eyes you can feel the beauty inside you,

Peaceful white, grounding brown and mesmerizing blue.

So, I put my camera and the canvas back in their place,

And I sat to watch you in awe existing in the evanescent space.

***

ANUPAM BANERJEE

Raju helped taking care of our home. Summers were spent in Mussoorie while the winters in Dehradun. Apart from his cooking, there are endless qualities about him, foremost being his honesty.

Raju

We were walking through the forest that day and leaves rustled beneath our feet,

A fresh feel of Autumn absorbed in the air and the aroma of pine oils in the breeze.

Our usual walk at five in the evening brought us new experiences every day,

There were bears and leopards in the forest but they never came our way.

It was in one of those walks sitting on a piece of stone underneath the Rhodendron,

I asked you how it was like to be in your village and describe where you came from.

You took a piece of twig from the ground and started to draw figures on the soil,

Four houses, a shop, a school, a river, on a mountain and a road with a coil.

You described this village as Chamba and it is famous for its scenic beauty,

Yours was a small house with cows, mountain goats, near a bee hive with honey.

Every morning the family went out in the forest to look for timber,

The earthen chulha in the home was lit up and rotis baked by your sister.

You showed me this plant called 'Bittchoo Booti' which stings if you touch it,

You said it is a delicacy you cook at home and enjoy with roti and salad.

You studied in a village school till class Eighth and then help at home,

Your father owned a tea stall which earned enough for 3 meals and 2 cups of tea alone.

There were five members in your family and so each had to contribute some earning,

Out in the sun doing farming of potatoes and ginger and selling them in the spring.

While in Mussoorie, a phone call to family every evening at Nine marks the end of your day,

Every year we parted for three months when the snow was thick and skies were grey.

Back at home you shoved off the snow and watched for bears attacking your livestock.

The time of the year when vegetables and tubers were stored along with wood-stock.

Every year in March you bring me white butter from your cow and a lot of mulberries,

They are best of all the things I have ever eaten along with yoghurt and raspberries.

I remember all those days and lot of images flash in my mind about your simplicity,

Your morning breakfast of Chai-Roti, never asking for a raise or gifts from me.

You know I like silence around the house so you spoke softly when you were near me.

How I miss those walks with you in the mountains and how I cherish your lovely tea.

15 years later

Years later you still call me so many times and we talk about your life back in the village,

You say things are better now as you have a new phone and sharing photos is a privilege.

We often talk about our time in Mussoorie and the places that have our memory,

You still ask me what I need from your village as you can send it across to me,

With these thoughts, the clock ticks eight and I slowly get up to prepare my morning tea.

***

Rains are on for long periods in Mussoorie. Endless cups of Chai and chatter mark the beginning and end of the day.

My house in Mussoorie

Its rainy season in Mussoorie,

My tin roof is drizzling aloud.

Water droplets tipper tapper,

Aided by a hailstone sound.

IN LIVING MEMORIES

I am at my window again,
The light bulb is bleak.
Fog covers the mountain,
I spot a bird with a wet beak.

In these times we feel cold,
And tell each other to be silent.
These sounds never get old,
And each time it feels different.

Our verandah is full with hailstones,
And it is a wonderful sight to see.
Hard on the outside but inside with varying tones,
They melt in my hand with glee.

After playing for some time, I return them,
Return them to the blissful grass outside.
Then step out to see the whole garden,
And walk on with a delightful stride.

We are looking forward to the afternoon,

There is going to be a special Puja they say.
We hear the distant drums and a sweet tune,
A chance visit to the local Goddess and pray.

After the ceremony we will be staying back,
There will be fables and tales from villagers.
Meanwhile we will peel potatoes from the sack,
Cooking a meal and distribute prasad to visitors.

These are the simple experiences we enjoy,
A community where people share and borrow.
The Sun will shine again and bring forth joy,
We are thankful for today and hopeful for tomorrow.

***

Narendranagar

A quaint town beset with Rishikesh in its front and a rich history, it is also home to a famous resort which offered me my first job.

In the simpleness of the mountain life and mundane life of the town dwellers, life prospers amongst a sunlit Himalayan view and natural waterfalls.

It rained last night. The air outside has mist droplets bristling with the cold October morning effect. With a weather change expected, I wear a jacket and carry an Umbrella with me.

Mornings in Narendranagar

It was still a foggy morning and the path curved on,

The incipient glow all around as the Sun looked upon.

The Himalayas were far, alit with a yellow highlight,

Resembling a diamond which is lovelier in moonlight.

Here I would walk up the mountain road up to my work,

Admiring the landscape around displayed as an artwork.

Sometimes the rain would drizzle in with a tipper tapper,

It would make us skip Umbrellas to hear the pitter patter.

IN LIVING MEMORIES

Stories of the past rang in my head which beautified these moments,

Listening slowly to the rain speak and gently answer my questions.

What a mystery the rain is;

It makes me happy on a few occasions,

and sometimes questions my decisions.

It brings me to the present and makes me happy suddenly,

and sometimes it fills me up with my past with melancholy.

If you keep trudging up, you will reach the Kunjapuri Temple,

Soak in the Holy smoke of the dhuni and receive grace in ample.

The eyes look far beyond to the mountains, houses, and streams,

An Eagle flies in the clear blue sky, the scene depicts my dreams.

The offering of flowers to the deity and tying the red kalava,

Feeling blessed eating Prasadam of Chole, bananas, and guava.

Climbing down through the stairs and looking back up again,

Thinking when will I be returning to feel uplifted and humane.

Thus, in the tipper tapper of the soft rains I walk on in life,

Singing my inner songs of peace shielding myself from strife.

***

One of the days at work. Learning happens in many ways.

This special day at "work"

As I walk through the market today,

I feel it is going to be a special day.

The cold morning and the fog clad mountain,

People sipping tea and feeling their palms dampen.

Vapors from hot tea on the wayside with butter bun,

Figures standing in corners soaking the morning sun.

I am tempted to hear those whispers,

Gossips and stories over a tea in whiskers.

But I do not have time as the clock is ticking,

A new job, expectations, a career in making.

I enter the work place and I find my boss waiting,

He looks at his clock and signals me to come in.

Being on time already feels like I am late,

"Hurry Anupam, its busy and no time to waste."

As I settled, I spotted a squirrel at the window side,

Quietly basking in the Sun rays from outside.

IN LIVING MEMORIES

I hear a loud thump of papers on my wooden desk,
"Anupam here is your task and today is another test,
With your remarkable abilities this is a piece of cake,
You will finish in no time and enjoy a long lunch break.
Showcase your smarts and complete these tasks today,
It is a great opportunity as your talents are on display."

"You are right Sir and I will take care of it right away,
Your appreciation has boosted me and made my day"

As soon as he left, I quickly reached out for my secret cupboard;
Hidden Cakes, coffee, biscuits covered and cluttered.
Knowing he will not be back until Eleven am so I have time to while away,
Still Seven in the morning and the Himalayas look mesmerizing today.

The sunshine, squirrel, and monkeys, are all around and with me,
We will complete the task together, after I finish my cake and coffee.

Just then the phone rang, "Anupam, I hope you are working on your tasks.

I will be in the morning meeting if anyone asks"

"Yes, Sir don't worry everything will be done on time"

My watch reads Eight Thirty am, and I do not have much time.

I know our Spa Reception opens at Nine am and there will be a huge onslaught of guests,

I will be running around here and there trying to pass too many tests.

So, I started on a task when suddenly couple of colleagues arrived,

Fresh morning jokes and stories of the last evening got me occupied.

Our talks went on until it was Ten Thirty am and suddenly there was a rush of panic,

Like Alice in Wonderland, my other self started warning me about the coming hours so tragic.

As I tried to focus, more colleagues came in and then a few guests,

Asking me questions and giving me new tests.

With that, the people started coming in and going,

I was speaking to them and conversations were flowing.

Twenty minutes left on the clock and the Boss was to arrive,

I tried to get to work but just then again, a few guests arrived.

I started talking to them about the Himalayan view outside,

And the large door opened on the other side.

I saw my boss enter, smiling, giving me a thumbs up,

I held my breath thinking now for sure I am in trouble.

I could not believe that he was happy and feeling great,

Did someone do the work on my behalf while I was late.

I smiled and closed my eyes, asking 'Who here is so kind and smart,

Who is my angel, reveal yourself my sweetheart?'

After the guest left, I started to complete my work hurriedly,

Then I went to my boss's office and entered his room slowly.

Thinking now I will be scolded for completing the work so late,

Instead, he smiled as he welcomed me in and offered me a chocolate.

So, he began the conversation saying, "I have been seeing you Mr. Banerjee

And I loved seeing the guests talk to you and they are so happy,

I am impressed with your work and your success stories,

You have miles to go and I see you doing well in this industry."

I said thank you very much and turned to come back to my desk,

I could not understand why I was praised when I had failed the test.

Then I asked myself what exactly is my "work" for which I had been praised?

And everything suddenly started making sense to my taste.

That we are hosts to the people who travel from far across the world,

They carry emotions and expectations depending on our word.

They are our guests and we share our life with them,

Life is a celebration and we participate in it with them.

How can we show someone else what is great in this moment?

If we would not know the gift we have in the form of the 'present.'

Thus, getting lost in the present, the laughs and conversations make sense,

I contributed to making someone happy with an unrequited expense.

So, the day was followed by more chats and more conversations,

I was happy all day with more laughter and more contributions.

***

Kuwait

Kuwait, a dream land for many and a comfortable abode for people who reach the gulf looking for jobs. Few pages are not enough to describe the magnitude of the Middle East. It must be experienced.

Heart notes of Kuwait

There are relationships you do not expect will happen,
Written on the sands of time, a story I have not forgotten.
The dazzling sea shore and dinner meets at the cornice,
Sharing meals and exchanging stories from far east.
People from varied cultures staying under one roof,
Different languages yet their smiles were a proof.
Smiles of instant connection, warmth, and friendship,
Helping each other to find their way on this starship.

My room was small with a diffused lighting,
Enough to store my beloved books and writings.
I reached the shores of Kuwait in early November,
Winter and the sky had a belated pink splendor.
First few days were settling in and visits to the bazaar,

Finding it hard to differentiate between 'Fils and Dinar.'
Shop owners, barbers, drivers from Iran and Pakistan,
A strange new land and my flat mate was from Oman.
A culture so mixed yet tied warmly to each other,
Separating us was only a label and a flag color.

My work place had people from different regions,
Unique countries, languages, and varied religions.

A natural connection is what I experienced right away,
Their welcome and willingness to help, allowed me to stay.
All the formalities and procedures - someone accompanied me always,
The mall, shopping and blending in, someone guided me the ways.
There were these days full of work when my mind wanted rest,
We went on walks after our shift for Coffee watching the sunset.

A middle eastern culture, the cuisine and watching lives,
Dinners, coffee, healthy dates, the 'Souq' and the drives.
In one of these drives, I saw a Cheetah as a pet in a car,
I looked twice to make sure but the car was not so far.
Yes, it was a Cheetah sitting in the middle of two guys,
Looking left and right at fast cars as he enjoyed the ride.

Bayan Palace is one of such colossal beauties of Kuwait,
Enigmatic charm, vibrant and an emblem of the state.
Upon entering, impressions of visitors displayed around,
Emirs, royals, dignitaries, Presidents, and all the renowned.
A great feeling prevails experiencing an artistic splendor,
Moments marveling over carvings in a sublime temper.

One of the famous markets is called Souq al Mubarakia,
A shopping hub for Kuwaitis, some streets ahead of Ikea.
Along with spices and vegetables, on sale are Arabic perfumes,
Mesmerized in the eminence and magnificence to presume.

Here you have cultures mix, open air exuberant restaurants,

Middle eastern cuisine, Sheesha and bakeries with Croissants.

One of these days it was when I was invited to a beach party,

A lot of people joining in a beautiful Yacht known as McCarty.

The pomp and show made me feel as if this is Tomorrowland,

Loud music, mocktails and luxuries, last minute and unplanned.

Of all the possibilities that the mind could fathom and guess,

Out came from one of the cabins, a one-year-old dusky lioness.

She mingled with everyone on board who called out her name,

Thinking of herself not more than a cat and was up for any game.

She was as thrilled and in enjoyment as the rest of us were,

Moments passed happily and it was next day when it was over.

I met people from Egypt working in various jobs in Kuwait,

A typical dialect and persona, all of them carried the same trait.

Easily distinguished, enterprising and hospitable to the core,

Karim, a server at the hotel café was a delight on the dance floor.

Getting used to Arabic people and their flowery Arabic accent,

They were overjoyed when I learnt a few words and I spoke them.

Everyone had a story to tell about their home and their past,

Goodbyes were difficult as we always thought this would last.

I remember I was told long back to be careful in Middle east,

That it is a foreign land with strict rules that are well policed.

But we are talking about human beings and they are the same,

With different cloaks and languages, separated only by name.

The method of connection stays constant in Kuwait or in Rome,

An embrace with a smile and a foreign country becomes home.

***

IN LIVING MEMORIES

There are days which remain special. Revisiting them in your mind does make you miss them because they leave you with a living memory for life.

It was that day

I see that day when I close my eyes,

Our laughs lit up the pretty pink skies.

The secret plan to go out for a lovely dinner,

One after another, events followed each other.

I could see you from a mile away, excited and waving,

I signaled you to look around as a car came honking.

These few hours felt like time was running out,

We wanted to visit every place we missed out.

The post lights and white sands looked different,

An evening corniche with a sea salt fragrance.

A cheerfulness amongst the crowd's murmur,

Everyone gazing at the waves and the surfer.

As the waves ushered forth the man loftily,

We all felt our slow breaths counting softly.

In his descent there was an ascent of delight,

The dusk slowly blending with the moonlight.

Feeling the dashes of water onwards we walked,
The transport was far away and so we talked.
How beautiful this whole year had been altogether,
All our meetings were a precious box full of treasure.

Not knowing if we would all be ever meeting again,
Friends forever and partners in mutual loss and gain.
How life brought us so far and the future it oversees,
This departure was difficult, that we would all agree.

We kept sharing past stories using "Remember?"
Our memories together since last September.

We kept walking till the last lamp-post and found a taxi,
Souq al Mubarakiya- Anupam, Jason, Kevin and Sonakshi.
The market had a different flavor as everything glittered,
Pointing out to each other new additions as time stickered.
We hurried to take our place at a crowded restaurant,

IN LIVING MEMORIES

The candle flickered and the air smelled light rose fragrant.

There were several discussions on the best dishes to order,

Secretly picking our favorites and knowing what to reorder.

Feeling so much in the present moment in this last evening,

Laughing but deeply feeling this friendship and its meaning.

We talked and stayed until the restaurant closed its doors,

Still up for Coffee and ice cream, we searched for stores.

A few were open so we bought and headed to the seaside,

We sat down looking at the half-moon and the high tide,

Knowing we might not see each other in our lives again,

These moments that made us feel thankful and complain.

Complain about not being sure if we can make promises,

Complain of the one short year passed in compromises.

Compromises of being in the present and forgetting tomorrow,

Compromises of risking to close our eyes, not expecting sorrow.

The times when our loud laughs occupied the whole day,
Jokes which carried no meanings made us smile all day.
This was the very spot we had our first meeting that day,
One year back, the sun was setting, Yes It was that day!
As we sat there that day sipping Coffee and looking far ahead,
There was a silence gripping us, no one heard anything or said.
Back in our rooms our baggage lay open waiting to be packed,
There was not enough room for the memories to be stacked.
Kevin had his flight the next day morning back to London,
He was presented a group photo framed beautifully by Jason.

We kept reminding each other about funny incidents and stories,
Still fresh in our minds, learning to live in Kuwait and our glories.

Thus, our talks went on through the night sitting at the Corniche,

We did not realize when it was Five am and time for our last wish.

So, standing up staring at the morning Sun we imagined a day,

Four of us, meeting again and the joy we would feel that day.

There will be a day when we will be laughing under the blue sky,

And our stories will continue forever and there shall be no goodbye.

Four years later (Anupam started working in Sri Lanka)

It had been four years since we had seen each other,

Yes, there were phone calls often but nothing further.

I had been missing this feeling all the while to reconnect,

Not satisfied with the occasional chats on the Internet.

A quondam emotion missing even though we moved on,

And I was sure I am not the only one feeling this so strong.

One day, as I opened my email there was mail from Kevin,

"What about a meetup," I smiled knowing what was coming.

Photos attached of our last day in Kuwait, sunset and the seaside,

A flash of memories, warmth and laughter, my eyes opened wide.

We all got together on a call and starting working on the date,

25th November 2016 in Sri Lanka, decided after lots of debate.

As the day was saved in my calendar and in my excited heart,

Scenes from our past kept appearing as flashbacks from the start.

Memories which were still so fresh and in time never forgotten,

Us four coming together again to celebrate this feeling begotten.

The meetup

So, the day arrived and we had all gathered for the meetup,

Sunset in background, the ocean and us, all were in the lineup.

Somethings had changed though as everyone were on their phones,

It took them sometime to absorb the moments and get into free flow.

As the moments soaked in and our breathing became slower,

We looked at each other and said "It was that day" and burst out in laughter.

We started talking and here we were living that day again in memory,

It was deeply felt as it had us all together flipping the mind image gallery.

Five days went by and each day was a profound experience,

We just got lost in the moments and in each other's presence.

Then the day arrived when we had to say good bye again,

IN LIVING MEMORIES

Sitting at the airport we had the same reasons to complain.

One year in Kuwait and now only five days together,

Will we ever get the chance to live in the same city forever.

I clearly saw us meeting again although I did not mention,

I am sure amongst all the sorrow we all had the same vision.

Cont...

So, standing up staring at the morning Sun we imagined a day,

Four of us, meeting again and the joy we would feel that day.

Under the blue skies we will be laughing and have so much to say,

Our stories will continue forever and again it will be that day.

***

Thailand

My travels across Thailand and long stays in distant parts have led me to see this country in a whole different perspective.

From hot geysers to ice cold medicinal streams, Thailand is much more than Bangkok and a country laden with treasures.

Chiang Mai, a beautiful town north of Thailand.

First few days in Chiang Mai

The clock ticks Four thirty and I arrive in Chiangmai,
A midafternoon rain molded the air humid and dry.
It was a short flight from New Delhi over the oceans,
Across the continent, a journey full of joy and emotions.

It was one of my trips outside India to a foreign land,
Carrying a hotel reservation and Thai Baht in my hand.
The taxi driver spoke in elementary English to me,
Kind and helpful, a grandfather aged all of sixty-three.

The check-in at the hotel was surprisingly warm and friendly,
Their smiles and welcome made me feel that they knew me.

With me well settled in my room and essentials stacked,
The next morning, I went on a walk after I unpacked.

On my way I heard gales of laughter and celebration,
It was Songkran, the water festival of the nation.
Children spraying each other with water from their toy guns,
Some of them throwing buckets of water on the run.
Out and out a colorless version of Holi in Thailand,
Tourists participate with water guns in their hand.
Although things were easy and I found my way around,
There is one thing which did not leave my mind's compound.
Indian food - the taste and the aroma of a Shahi Paneer and Roti,
The sumptuous usual preparations and our most beloved Khichri.
I did find an Indian Restaurant serving all these dishes,
It was not the same as in India amongst a lot of other misses.
Thai food is much more varied than the famous Pad Thai noodle,

With fresh organic ingredients, beautiful flavorings, despite being frugal.

The roads are encouraging as they have well planned rules in traffic,

Hire a bike or cycle and the whole of Chiangmai seems charismatic.

All in all, a wonderful little town surrounded by hills and temples,

A feel of the real Thailand with villages around and a life so simple.

A mountain track with a night long train ride takes you to Bangkok,

Sweet memories of Chiangmai and new experiences to unlock.

***

Doi Inthanon is the highest mountain in Thailand. This story is about my dive into a fresh water stream.

Doi Inthanon

It was my first deep dive into wild waters,
The clear sunlight reaching the far bottom.
While inside I looked far outside the waters,
Lovely trees surround and flowers blossom.

Feeling akin to this world which is at peace,
A slow rhythm abounds without a timepiece.
Fishes swimming all around in this green haze,
Crabs perched under the rocks forming a maze.
The river weeds flow in a pattern of left and right,
Flashing and obscuring the turtles from my sight.

In that moment I felt in control of an ecosystem,
Land and now water, a newly gained wisdom.
Just then I felt a light wave push me forward,
I tried to feel the ground but my feet felt awkward.
Having nothing to hold on to instilled an insecurity,

IN LIVING MEMORIES

Suddenly I started struggling for breath with severity.
A small whirlpool inside the water pulled me in,
The clear waters had me in a deadlock and chagrin.
I found myself being carried away against my will,
Downstream, slowly and challenging my survival skill.

Nonplussed and wilted with an incipient lack of hope,
I gave more and more tries to reach the nearest rope.
It felt like an entire life worth of strength to save my life,
Swimming upstream, thoughts of drowning were rife.

Just then as though with a miracle I reached a rock,
Clenching it strongly, I recovered from a shock.
Gasping for air I felt a difference in temperature,
With a blood rush my face was hot;
While my feet were freezing cold as if in a refrigerator.

With these anomalies of feelings, I slowly climbed up,
The feeling of being alive struck me and I lapped it up.
Breathing deep, I looked around the forest and the stream,

It still looked innocent and inviting in its charming gleam.

My heart was beating fast trying to recover from the horror,

I did not step back into the water and feigned to be an explorer.

I do not blame the water or myself for this experience,

It was a stroke of luck that a learning was part of this experience.

I withdrew and became still inside my mind.

I was thankful to be breathing again,

And thankful to be given life again.

***

This is the story of Kasem from Chiangmai. I met him while staying at a resort in Koh Samui in Thailand and one pleasant afternoon he shared his life story with me.

Throwing stones in the river

Kasem-

It was a lone cloudy afternoon,

Sometime in the month of June.

IN LIVING MEMORIES

A letter, the postman came to deliver,
And I sat throwing stones in the river.

My friend was working in a resort,
A place which was heaven in short.
Beautiful water villas and the ocean,
Silent sunsets holding the horizon.
I wished to work here once in my life,
Word about its prominence was rife.

I was beginning to see changes around me,
Facebook and Internet, was all new to me.
I also wanted to go in town to make money,
My neighbors were prospering in my vicinity.

I possessed a variety of assumption and doubts,
My simplicity was different from the crowds.
Yes, I believed in my honesty and hard work,
Never the one to abandon duties and shirk.

I had asked my friend to get me a job with him,

IN LIVING MEMORIES

Starting to earn after high school was the maxim.

He assured me to not worry and that he will help me,

The thought of leaving home was a bit quaint for me.

The postman delivered my letter of appointment,

The resort called me to confirm my employment.

I was ravished with joy and sadness together,

My home and my chicken pen were my treasure.

But I had made up my mind to go out in the world,

To understand its functioning and why it swirled.

On a slow chugging train and partly on the boat,

I travelled watching sunsets drifting on the moat.

I was feeling a sense of faith in my abilities,

And clearly aware of my family responsibilities.

Upon reaching the resort gates I was astounded,

The magnanimity of it all left me dumbfounded.

With a bag in my hand, I was ushered in silently,

People in uniforms, polite and smiling patiently.

Someone showed me my room and the dining hall,

And asked me if I was fine and needing anything at all.
I was suddenly feeling relaxed and at ease,
I went to rest after collecting my locker keys.

Six months later

The last six months have been the best in my life,
and again, there was a birthday party last night.
They gave me a room housekeeping attendant job,
It was the season time, lot of work and occupancy bob.
I must admit that I had to learn and persevere,
With a supportive environment, I could pioneer.

Now I have money to send home to my mother,
My sister's wedding is soon round the corner.
I am proud that it is happening so soon,
Blessed with the auspicious monsoon.

And I cannot wait to return home and tell my stories,
I learnt so much and made beautiful new memories.
I learned to speak English and improve every day,
And I also have a French and carpentry class today.

Every night after my duty we share moments in leisure,

We chat with friends and make vacation plans together.

Life goes by laughing and telling stories to each other,

Sometimes I go for walks alone;

And sometimes I sit throwing stones in the river.

***

From the poet's pen

Few of my selected poems for you...

Maggi in the mountains

Here comes my vaporous Maggi,
Lip smacking, spicy and taggy.
My eyes look far ahead in the valley,
Through a translucent steam rally.

I enjoy a plain one in its originality,
A timeless gratifying specialty.
My friend orders a vegetable one,
It arrives flavory but overdone.
Sipping in hot tea hand pressed,
Anomalies are put to good rest.

We begin a conversation on wolves,
Stories on notorious werewolves.
These hills have hidden mysteries,
Tales of people and their histories.

Just then we saw a flying squirrel,
He dashed to a tree in a quarrel.
Being followed by his little brother,
For a piece of fig, they saw together.
His tiny forepaw grabbed the fruit,
While the brother was in pursuit.
Off they began their sweet tug of war,
Both sides quivering;
A reward they both had fallen for.
Alas, the little one loses the battle,
The fruit goes to the winner's saddle.
Although there was another fig nearby,
The little one waited patiently hereby.
The big brother ate half and sprinted away,
Leaving the rest of the fig for the little one;
And to enjoy the wonderful day.

I am then reminded by my friend to move,
The orange Sun is setting down the groove.
There is a forest rest house hosting us tonight,

Charcoal lit food and stories will fill the night.

So, hoping for an evening full of splendors,

We ride up the ridge for more adventures.

***

Momos or Dumplings were a huge part of our childhood. The authentic quality of Tibetan Momo in Rajpur carry generations of secret flavors and taste which stamps you with one of the unforgettable experiences of Dehradun.

Momo

You know that I love you,

I know you love me too.

IN LIVING MEMORIES

You find me everywhere,
Whether in joy or despair.
Out of the blue and like magic,
Your great pull is automatic.

Our first meeting at Bhutia Market in Nainital,
The day I skipped Rice and Dal.
Twenty-five years ago, and the memory is clear,
Not one but two plates quickly disappeared.
My tongue relished that taste which was strange,
I never had something so simple but an outrange.

In the first plate you arrived raw and "steamy,"
In the next one you were fried and "creamy."
I was perplexed as to which shall I call best,
Trying not to be biased and make you upset.
Both were yummy with a red chili chutney,
Bringing good feelings, making my nose runny.
So, I decided I will have you both anytime I do,
And our love shall remain safe between me and you.

IN LIVING MEMORIES

All the gym trainers and dieticians,

All the doctors and mathematicians,

Could not keep me away from you,

Even without the chutney I love you.

I am so lucky to be in Dehradun,

With friends who love you too.

Tomorrow is Tsering's birthday,

Which means a happy Momo Day.

I close my eyes and think about you,

It seems your Aunty is my favorite too.

Her name is Thukpa and she is healthy,

Noodles, meat, and vegetables wealthy.

Here I am this afternoon again having skipped Rice and Dal

Its cold outside, the Sun and its heat are very far.

Out you come from the steamer with all that fat,

A soup, chutney, garlic vinegar and all of that.

IN LIVING MEMORIES

I burst you open after dipping you in a red chutney,
Carefully curated with love feels like my mouth is honey.

Soft and plump melting readily without doubt,
You are deliciously hot as I cover my mouth.
This one piece takes a while to chew and dissolve,
All in all, a mystery and I have seven more to solve.

After three plates of you I am still not fulfilled,
My stomach fights with my mind;
Seeing your magical powers, I am thrilled.
You remained an unsolved mystery impossible to decode,
Curious again, I am looking forward to the next episode.
I will return next week and surely solve you,
But I know that I am in an unsolvable romance with you.

The next week, I arrive looking vehemently at the Menu,
Trying not to look at your name and cleverly tease you.
As I read Shaptak and Tingmo, Khapse and Thenthuk,
And then the mighty Rhe chotse and Tsam thuk.
As I tried to make up my mind the server approached me,

Seeing me in a fix said "Sir is it the same like always - Momo and red chutney?"

At first, I said 'no' trying not to think of Momo but the image flashed in my mind,

It feels like a century since I had you and I could feel my saliva rapidly grind.

So, I gave up again and ordered three plates of you which I ate with relish,

Some soft drink alongside which the Mussoorie mountains helped me cherish.

During departure, feeling guilty I asked the cook if he can make me other dishes next time which look great too,

He said 'Yes, just order from the menu,'

But in my mind, I know I will come back secretly looking only for you.

***

Travelling towards Dhanaulti, on the hill road many a Maggi, Omelet and Tea shops prosper. Some experiences are more than just a meal.

Tea on the mountain road

We are in the hills after travelling far and long,

The same feeling of 'this is where I truly belong'.

It seems like a painting how the sun is gleaming,

The mist tries to hide it but instead its redeeming.

From a point behind the mountain;

The Sun spreads like a fountain,

It is a moment which captures me;

In my mind a serenity touches me.

This vacant road climbing a curvy path uphill,

They are as empty as my eyes chasing freewill.

Children in red sweaters returning from school,

Walking in line to their village with a home rule.

Oh, look there is a child trying to sell us berries,

Sprinkled with Himalayan salt, lovely red raspberries.

His smile is a story of a family waiting back home,

He must sell the berries and buy food for home.

Then there is a boy making Omelet, Bread, and Tea,
He smiles at our camera thankful for the opportunity.
A family of seven people who depend on his income,
A year of low harvest, not enough Ginger, and Plum.

As we spent some time sitting and soaking the beauty,
More children arrived owning bags of berries and sooty.
The same exhilaration and expectant smile on their faces,
Hiding their burden of family living in hemmed in places.

An air of wonder and a hidden heartfelt envy in me,
Startled at seeing people happy with needs so elementary.
A life without reasoning, debates and relying on books,
They are content and convinced in sitting by the brooks.
A morning beginning with chickens clucking away at five,
An evening which ends with chats from the history archive.
They rely on old adages passed down from their grandmother,

Recipes of local herbs, vegetables, and spices of rainbow color.

Being in the moment, living without worrying about tomorrow,

Enough for everyone through generations without grief and sorrow.

Thus, I thought about my life and why am I searching for happiness,

Why I don't have a life like these people as my life seems meaningless.

Just then I saw a group of tourists arrive and the boys rushing to them,

To sell their berries, I saw an intense fight and mayhem amongst them.

The smiling and kindly humans suddenly turned into fierce beings,

Their focus was money and they seemed not to see or be hearing.

A reality dawned on me on their daily struggle to maintain their home,

Struggling every day and crossing mountains where their goats roam.

We all have different journeys, unique milestones, and distinct walkways,

There is no need to compare as we all are gifted with our own doorways.

Suffice it is to realize what we possess and count these as life's blessings,

Being happy and content with the treasure life gave us and its meanings.

Thus, I looked back upon my life and suddenly felt a spring of beatitude,

I started my bike with zest to reach the forest rest house on a high altitude.

From then on there was a gleam and shine around me in a natural splendor,

That tea on the mountain road and its flavor carried gratitude and surrender.

***

Hussein, the Barber

Slow but definite, sweeping across invisible lines,
Hussein uses his scissors and blade in great confines.
His refined eyes set on the area which he earmarked,
Passion brought him far and got his name trademarked.

Generations of barbers from the time of Rajas until today,
A family tradition and a pride are evident and on display.
The ability to make someone look different and feel great,
A silent confidence knowing the design he will create.

A weary client comes in having escaped the noise of the city,
He has chosen his peace with a simple cut and shave being witty.
For an hour, this therapy will proceed to relax him further,
He switched off his cell phone to be undisturbed in slumber.
He knows that this hour is his personal space and a golden hour,
A time he treasures amongst his daily duties of grinding flour.

This time gives him a feeling of not being controlled by anyone,

The pleasure of being alone without demands from someone.

With sharp eyes the barbers' hands slide definite and strong,

Seeing his client relax, he himself is at ease and sings a song.

The song serves as a lullaby for the reclined guest on the seat,

The rustling sound of the blade is cushioned by lather and heat.

He loves feeling lightheaded getting out of the barbershop,

Anticipating appreciation for his new hair cut in talks;

he will eavesdrop.

Hussein is aware of the trust that is placed in his knowledge,

The method of his head massage was invented in his own college.

The headache which troubled his client since morning is now gone,

The cool nourishing hair oil transcends tranquility and beyond.

As Hussein finishes his appointment at One pm and prepares for lunch,

He folds the towels neatly, hangs the apron and wipes off the grunge.

Having a meal is sacred behind closed doors sitting down on the floor,

Talks of mundane life, some news and list of things to do as part of chore.

The day ends at Eight pm with an area clean up and counting the till,

The door is bolted shut and prayers of thanks are offered being still.

Hussein will wake up at Five am tomorrow and his beliefs are from the old school,

He questions the meaning of depression and why you swim in a swimming pool.

In his days he swam the ravaging rivers in the south which were wide and deep,

Taking care of his goats and land all day, then Nine pm was the time to go to sleep.

He says in his self-convinced words that your life will be healthy if you get up early,

He is unhappy to see young kids going to sleep when he wakes up at Five to make tea.

His elder children have finished college and moved to big cities for jobs,

He is content where he is, working as he does and he does not like snobs.

Hussein returns home at Eight Thirty,

Relishes Kebabs and Roti.

The radio plays yesteryear songs,

He sits eyes closed and sings along.

Pouring water from the earthen pitcher,

He smiles watching his asleep granddaughter.

GLOSSARY

Reference: Merriam Websters and Google Dictionaries.

Adage - A saying often in metaphorical form that typically embodies a common observation. She reminded him of the adage: "A penny saved is a penny earned."

Analogy – A comparison of two otherwise unlike things based on resemblance of a particular aspect

Anomaly- Something different, abnormal, peculiar

Beatitude- A state of utmost bliss

Beckon - Make a gesture with the hand, arm, or head to encourage or instruct someone to approach or follow

Begotten-Brought into existence by or as if by a parent

Belated- Coming or happening later than should have been the case.

Bichu Buti Saag- A dish made from 'Stinging nettle' plant which grows wild in the hills esp. in Uttarakhand.

Benign- Showing kindness and gentleness

Bob- Make a quick, short movement up and down.

Burble -To make a bubbling sound

Burrow- A hole or tunnel dug by a small animal, especially a rabbit, as a dwelling.

Canister- A round or cylindrical container used for storing such things as food, chemicals, or rolls of film.

Chagrin- Distress of mind caused by humiliation, disappointment, or failure.

Chulha - A small earthen or brick stove used most in villages.

Chutney - A spicy condiment of Indian origin, made of fruits or vegetables and spices.

Colossal - Extremely large or great.

Culminate- Reach a climax or point of highest development

Curator -One who has the care and superintendence of something

Dal – Lentil Curry

Dainty -Marked by delicate beauty, form, or grace

Dash -To move with sudden speed

Disquiet- to take away the peace or tranquillity of

Ebb and flow -used to describe something that changes in a regular and repeated way

Enamour - Be filled with love for.

Evanescent- Soon passing out of sight, memory, or existence; quickly fading or disappearing.

Exuberant - Full of energy, excitement, and cheerfulness.

Feign - To give a false appearance of

Frenzied - Wildly excited or uncontrolled.

Frugal - Simple and costing little.

Gleam – A small bright light

Haze - Fine dust, smoke
Hemmed in - to surround in a restrictive manner
Incipient - Beginning to come into being or to become apparent
Jaan – Darling / Life
Jubilant -Feeling or expressing great happiness and triumph
Marvel- Be filled with wonder or astonishment
Maxim- A general truth, fundamental principle, or rule of conduct
Mayhem- Needless or wilful damage or violence
Maze - Something confusingly elaborate or complicated
Meadow – A piece of grassland, near a river
Melancholy -Sadness or depression of mind or spirit
Melee- A situation in which a crowd of people are in a hurry or pushing each other in a confused way
Mesmerizing - Capturing one's complete attention as if by magic.
Obscure - Hidden by darkness
Onslaught - An especially fierce attack
Pahadi Rajma – Kidney Beans grown in mountains.
Pariah – A breed used to define the Indian street dogs.
Perch- A resting place
Planks - A long, thin, flat piece of timber
Puddle -A small pool of liquid, especially of rainwater on the ground.

Quaint -Unusual or different in character or appearance
Quiver- To shake or move with a slight trembling motion
Quondam - That once was
Ravish -To overcome with emotion (such as joy or delight)
Replicate -Make an exact copy of; reproduce
Reprimand - Criticism for a fault
Requite - To make return for.
Revelation - The act of revealing or disclosing
Reminisce - Indulge in enjoyable recollection of past events.
Saag - Spinach or another leafy vegetable.
Sculpted face - A part of someone's face or body that is sculpted is very firm or straight in an attractive way
Shaan – Pride
Shroud – A thing that envelops or obscures something.
Slime -Soft moist
Slither -To slip or slide
Snout - The projecting nose and mouth of an animal, especially a mammal
Splendour- Magnificent and splendid appearance
Splendour-Great brightness.
Splinter-A small, thin, sharp piece of wood, glass, or similar material broken off from a larger piece.
Stride- Walk with long, decisive steps in a specified direction
Strife - Bitter sometimes violent conflict

Sublime- Of very great excellence or beauty.
Sumptuous -Extremely costly, rich, luxurious, or magnificent
Taggy- Full of or matted into tags (as of wool)
Tamatar -Tomato
Tread- walk in a specified way.
Trudge -To walk or march steadily and usually laboriously
Unravel -solve a puzzle
Vagrant -A person without a settled home or regular work who wanders from place to place
Vehement- Marked by forceful energy
Vicinity - **A** surrounding area or district
Whisker - Any of the long, stiff hairs growing on the face of a cat, mouse, or other mammal
Zest- An enjoyably exciting quality

THANK YOU FOR BEING WITH ME!

About me

I am a full-time dreamer of rainbows and miracles and I believe that they can be manifested. I love spending time in nature and experiencing life as it is. Poetry came to me naturally when I realized that I had run short of words to explain experiences in my life so I sought minimum words to communicate utmost emotions. This is my first book and I hope to see you in my world soon, again.

Yours,

Anupam

www.ingramcontent.com/pod-product-compliance
Lightning Source LLC
LaVergne TN
LVHW052050160826
845678LV00015B/3158

* 9 7 8 9 3 5 6 7 3 3 6 6 4 *